THE YOUNG PERSON'S GUIDE TO

SHAKESPEARE

THE YOUNG PERSON'S GUIDE TO

SHAKESPEARE

IN ASSOCIATION WITH

THE ROYAL SHAKESPEARE COMPANY

WITH SPOKEN WORD FROM THE PLAYS

BOOK WRITTEN BY

ANITA GANERI

PAVILION

First published in Great Britain in 1999 by
PAVILION BOOKS LTD
London House, Great Eastern Wharf
Parkgate Road, London SW11 4NQ

Copyright © Pavilion Books 1999
Text copyright © Anita Ganeri 1999
For copyright of photographs, see p.53

Consultant: Kathy Elgin, Royal Shakespeare Company
Designer: Nigel Partridge
Editor: Jo Fletcher-Watson

A CIP catalogue record for this book is available
from the British Library

ISBN 1 86205 156 9

Set in ITC Garamond
Printed in China

2   4   6   8   10   9   7   5   3   1

This book can be ordered direct from the publisher.
Please contact the Marketing Department.
But try your bookshop first.

*Frontispiece: The final scene from the RSC's 1991 production
of* Much Ado About Nothing

Contents

Introduction

A great welcome to the fascinating world of William Shakespeare! In Shakespeare's time, going to the theatre was the most popular form of entertainment, as going to the cinema or watching a sports event is today. Almost 400 years later, Shakespeare's plays are still incredibly popular all over the world, making him the most performed, printed, and translated playwright ever. His work has inspired many films, plays, and books, bringing his beautiful language and finely drawn plots and characters to a new modern audience. His work is read by millions of students in schools and universities all over the world.

This book looks at Shakespeare's life in Stratford and London, and at his flourishing career, first as an actor, then as a playwright. Read about Shakespeare's major works and meet his most famous characters. Find out how Shakespeare is performed in the theatre, from the selection of a play to the rising curtain on opening night. The accompanying CD includes recordings of actors performing some of Shakespeare's most famous speeches, which are also printed on pages 50–52. *The Young Person's Guide to Shakespeare* is the perfect introduction to the life and work of the world's most beloved playwright.

LEFT: *A scene from* The Tempest *by the Cuban Theatre Company at the Teatro Buendía*

Who Was Shakespeare?

William Shakespeare wrote some of the most famous plays and poems in the English language. His beautiful language and universal themes of love, ambition, and jealousy make his work as popular and relevant today as when it was written nearly 400 years ago.

When did Shakespeare live?

Shakespeare lived from 1564 to 1616 in England, during the reigns of Elizabeth I (1558–1603) and James I (1603–1625). It was a golden age for theatregoing. Many actors became rich and famous. The first permanent theatres in London were built, and audiences flocked to the plays. There was plenty of work for aspiring playwrights, especially those as gifted as Shakespeare. This was also the golden age of exploration, when sailors and traders from Europe ventured into undiscovered parts of the world. The name of Shakespeare's theatre, the Globe, reflected that spirit of adventure.

A well-known portrait of Shakespeare, painted by John Taylor

What do we know about Shakespeare?

There are very few written records about Shakespeare or his family. None of the original manuscripts of his plays, poems, or sonnets has survived. The only remaining examples of Shakespeare's own handwriting are six versions of his signature, from his will and other legal documents.

FAR LEFT: A more romantic portrayal of Shakespeare, painted by Soest

LEFT: Queen Elizabeth I

Performing Shakespeare

All over the world, Shakespeare's plays are performed more often than those of any other playwright in history. They have influenced hundreds of films, musicals, ballets, and operas. More than 300 film versions of the major plays have been produced. Playing a Shakespearean role is often the greatest challenge of an actor's career.

Shakespeare's Early Life

Shakespeare, the third of eight children, was born in Stratford-upon-Avon, a market town in Warwickshire, England. His father, John, was a glovemaker and a dealer in wool and property. His mother, Mary Arden, was the daughter of a wealthy local landowner.

Shakespeare's school days

From the age of eleven onward, Shakespeare probably attended King Edward VI Grammar School in Stratford. Here he developed his love of literature, both ancient and modern, which later served him well in his work as a playwright. Around the age of fifteen, he left school and started working for his father. He did not pursue a university education.

The Henley Street house where Shakespeare was born

SHAKESPEARE'S STRATFORD

Many of the places associated with the life of Shakespeare in Stratford have been preserved and can be visited today.

◆ **SHAKESPEARE'S BIRTHPLACE**
The Henley Street house where Shakespeare was born. Part of the house is furnished as it would have been in Shakespeare's time.

◆ **NEW PLACE AND NASH'S HOUSE**
Shakespeare's family home from 1597 until his death. Only the site and foundation remain. Next door is Nash's House, which belonged to Thomas Nash, who was the first husband of

ABOVE: *The schoolroom of King Edward VI Grammar School, Stratford, as it would have been in Shakespeare's day*

DID YOU KNOW?

Traditionally, Shakespeare's birthday is celebrated as April 23, 1564, although we do not know the exact date on which he was born. Coincidentally, he died on April 23, 1616.

Shakespeare's only granddaughter, Elizabeth.

◆ **HALL'S CROFT**
The home of Shakespeare's daughter Susanna and her husband, Dr. John Hall, before they moved to New Place after Shakespeare's death

◆ **ANNE HATHAWAY'S COTTAGE**
Anne's home before her marriage, in the village of Shottery, near Stratford

◆ **MARY ARDEN'S HOUSE**
The farmhouse where Shakespeare's mother grew up, in the village of Wilmcote, near Stratford

Anne Hathaway's cottage

DID YOU KNOW?

Before permanent theatres began to be built in London in the 1570s, groups of actors travelled from town to town performing the latest plays. When Shakespeare's father was mayor of Stratford, he encouraged these companies to perform in the town. Shakespeare would have seen these plays, which may have inspired his love of theatre.

Getting married

On November 27, 1582, at age eighteen, Shakespeare married Anne Hathaway, the daughter of a farmer from nearby Shottery. She was eight years older than he and pregnant at the time of their marriage. Their first daughter, Susanna, was christened on May 26, 1583. Two years later Anne gave birth to twins, Hamnet and Judith. Hamnet died in 1596, at age eleven.

The lost years

By 1592 Shakespeare had left Stratford for London and was making his name as an actor and playwright. We do not know what happened in the so-called lost years before that, between 1585 and 1592. According to various stories, Shakespeare worked as a schoolmaster, soldier, or lawyer, or he joined a touring company of actors visiting Stratford.

Shakespeare in London

In Shakespeare's day, London was a thriving city of nearly 200,000 people. It was crowded and dirty, with great contrast between the lives of rich and poor. On arriving in London, Shakespeare found lodgings in Bishopsgate, then moved to Bankside, to be closer to the theatres.

The first theatres

The first permanent indoor theatre building was constructed in Shoreditch, in east London, in 1576. It was called The Theatre. Before this, plays were often performed in the yards of taverns and inns. In 1587 the Rose Theatre was built in Bankside, followed by the Swan (1594–1595) and the Globe (1599). The Swan, which held 3,000 people, was described as the biggest and finest theatre in London.

A painting of London in the 1600s viewed from the south bank of the Thames

ENTERTAINMENTS

In addition to the theatre, the Elizabethans loved bear- and bull-baiting, cockfighting, and watching public executions. This is how one eyewitness described a visit to the Bear Garden in Bankside:

"There is a round building, three stories high, in which are kept about a hundred large English dogs, with separate wooden kennels for each of them. These dogs were made to fight singly with three bears, the second bear being larger than the first and the third larger than the second. After this, a bull was brought in and chased by the dogs, and at last a bull who defended himself most bravely."

Bear-baiting was a brutal but popular Elizabethan pastime.

ABOVE: What the Rose Theatre would have looked like in Shakespeare's day. The raised flag indicates that a play is about to begin.

RIGHT: An artist's impression of London's south bank in Elizabethan times, showing the position of the theatres

DID YOU KNOW?

To cross the river to the theatres, people could hail a small ferry boat, called a wherry. They knew which way the boat was heading by the ferryman's cry of "Westward ho!" or "Eastward ho!" A plan to move the theatres north of the river was blocked by the ferrymen because such a move would have been bad for their business.

Bankside

The theatres were deliberately built outside the walls of the city of London in order to remain outside the strict control of the city authorities, who claimed that plays had a bad effect on people's morals. Bankside, close to London Bridge on the south bank of the Thames, was notorious for its brothels, gambling dens, taverns, and low life.

Actors' companies

Each theatre had its own company of actors and was sponsored by a wealthy patron. Shakespeare joined the Lord Chamberlain's Men. In 1603 the company became the King's Men, with King James himself as their patron. Shakespeare worked first as an actor and director, and later as chief playwright. Along with the other leading actors, he also owned shares in the company and in the Globe Theatre.

The Great Wooden O

In 1599 Shakespeare and the Lord Chamberlain's Men took up residence in a new theatre on Bankside. It was called the Globe. *As You Like It* is thought to have been their first production.

Building the Globe

The Globe was built from the timbers of The Theatre in Shoreditch, the previous home of the Lord Chamberlain's Men. The landlord had refused to renew the lease, so under cover of night, the actors dismantled The Theatre beam by beam, secretly ferried it across the river, and had it rebuilt in Bankside. Because it was partly open to the sky, the Globe could be used only in summer. From October to April, when the Globe was closed, the Globe's actors performed in an indoor playhouse at Blackfriars.

What the Globe looked like

In the prologue to *Henry V*, Shakespeare himself describes the Globe as "this wooden O." In fact, the theatre was not completely round but had five sides. It was half-timbered, with a thatched roof above the more expensive gallery seats. Around the stage was the open yard where audience members called groundlings could stand and watch the play. The stage, sheltered by an ornate ceiling, extended into the middle of the yard, so the groundlings were always closest to the action. The staging area probably had trapdoors in the flooring and primitive rigging overhead. When full, the theatre held around 2,500 people.

The original Globe, as it appeared in Claus Jan Visscher's View of London, *in 1616*

An artist's impression of Queen Elizabeth I watching The Merry Wives of Windsor *inside the Globe Theatre*

Disaster strikes

On June 29, 1613, during a performance of *Henry VIII*, disaster struck. A cannon on the stage backfired and set the thatched roof on fire. In less than an hour, the theatre burned to the ground. Incredibly, no one was hurt, though one man's breeches caught on fire! The Globe was rebuilt in 1614 and was soon back in business. But it was closed by the Puritans in 1642 and demolished two years later.

The new Globe, London

EYEWITNESS ACCOUNT

Sir Henry Wotton, an eyewitness to the Globe fire, described the event in a letter to a friend:

"Certain cannons being shot off at [King Henry's] entry, some of the Paper, or other stuff wherewith one of them was stopped, did light on the Thatch, where . . . it kindled inwardly, and ran round like a train, consuming within less than an hour the whole house to the very ground. This was the fatal period of that vertuous Fabrique; wherein nothing did perish, but Wood and Straw, and a few forsaken Cloaks."

The new Globe

In 1996, just a stone's throw away from the site of the original theatre, a brand-new Globe opened its doors to the public. The brainchild of American actor and director Sam Wanamaker, it took almost ten years to build. Contemporary audiences can now see Shakespeare's plays performed in the theatre for which they were written.

A Visit to the Theatre

Elizabethans flocked to the theatre to see the latest plays and to cheer or boo the actors. The most popular form of entertainment at the time, theatregoing was for everyone, ordinary people as well as wealthy ones.

Performance times

Because the theatres had no artificial lighting, performances were held in the afternoon, beginning at 2:00 P.M. A silk flag was flown above the theatre to show that a performance would be staged that day. Just before the play began, a trumpet was blown to hurry theatregoers along. There were performances every day of the year, except on Sundays and during Lent.

A painting of Elizabethans enjoying a visit to the Globe in Shakespeare's time, by George Pycroft

All the world's a stage,
And all the men and women merely
*   players.*
They have their exits and their
*   entrances,*
And one man in his time plays
*   many parts,*
His acts being seven ages.
*   Jaques,* As You Like It, *Act II,*
*   sc. vii, 139–143*

You can listen to this speech on
the CD.

An artist's impression of the Rose
Theatre after alterations in 1592

Seats and prices

The cheapest tickets cost a penny. This bought standing room in the yard around the stage, where the groundlings stood. For twopence you could sit in the lower gallery. Sixpence bought a seat in the upper gallery or on the stage itself. A "gentleman's room," or box, cost one shilling, which was a lot of money at the time.

Audience participation

Elizabethan audiences were not as well behaved as modern theatregoers. They talked, ate, and drank throughout the play, sang along to the songs, and sometimes even jumped onto the stage and joined in the swordfights. If they did not like what they saw, they booed and threw rotten fruit at the actors!

DID YOU KNOW?

A group of actors called gatherers stood at theatre doors to collect the ticket money, which was then locked away in a box. This is where we get the term *box office*, what we call a theatre ticket office today.

An Actor's Life

Being an actor in Shakespeare's day was very hard work. Each company put on several plays a week, and an actor rarely performed the same role for two days in a row.

Becoming an actor

Many actors started in children's companies. Others went straight into adult companies, between the ages of ten and thirteen. Women were not allowed to act, so female parts were played by young boys. Most actors had little training, though some were apprenticed to senior actors. There was a strict pecking order. At the bottom were the boy apprentices. Then came the "hired men," who acted as extras and backstage staff. At the top were the "sharers," who had money invested in the company.

In this authentic Elizabethan production of Henry V *at the new Globe, London, Princess Katharine and the French Queen are both played by men.*

DID YOU KNOW?

Many actors were paid less than 10 shillings a week, but written into their contracts was a list of heavy fines for breaking the rules:
- 1 shilling for arriving late at rehearsals
- 2 shillings for missing a rehearsal
- 3 shillings for not being ready, in costume, to start a performance
- 10 shillings for being drunk onstage
- 20 shillings for missing a performance
- 40 pounds for stealing a costume

Life's but a walking shadow, a poor player
That struts and frets his hour upon the stage,
And then is heard no more.
    Macbeth, Macbeth, *Act V, sc. v,*
        23–25

DID YOU KNOW?

Shakespeare acted in his own plays and also in those of other playwrights, such as Ben Jonson. He seemed satisfied to play minor roles, such as Adam, the servant in *As You Like It,* and the ghost of Hamlet's father.

Richard Burbage

THEATRE PROPS

Little scenery was used onstage. Instead, elaborate costumes and props set the scene. While no records of the Globe's props remain, an inventory exists from the Rose:
◆ Item, 1 rock, 1 cage, 1 tomb, 1 Hell Mouth
◆ Item, 2 steeples, and 1 chime of bells, and 1 beacon
◆ Item, 1 Globe, and 1 golden sceptre; 3 clubs
◆ Item, 2 marchpanes and the city of Rome
◆ Item, 1 Golden fleece, 2 rackets, 1 bay tree
◆ Item, 1 wooden canopy; old Mahomet's head
◆ Item, 8 vizards (masks)
◆ Item, Cupid's bow, and quiver; the cloth of the sun and moon
◆ Item, 2 mossy banks and one snake

Leading actors

The most famous actors in Shakespeare's company included:
RICHARD BURBAGE (1567–1619)
Sharer, manager, and leading actor of tragic roles.
Shakespeare wrote many of his tragic heroes, including Hamlet, Macbeth, Othello, and Richard III, especially for Burbage.

NATHAN FIELD (1587–1620)
An actor and playwright who started his career in a children's company. Field took Shakespeare's place in the King's Men in 1615. He wrote two plays of his own and collaborated on others.

WILLIAM KEMPE (? –1603)
The main comedian in the company. Kempe played clowns and fools, including Dogberry in *Much Ado About Nothing*. He left the Lord Chamberlain's Men in 1599, perhaps because Shakespeare did not like his habit of making up his own lines instead of reciting those that had been written!

Nathan Field

An actor's day

Actors worked incredibly hard. With so many plays to perform, there was little time to learn lines or rehearse. In addition to having excellent memories, actors were also expected to sing, dance, play musical instruments, and fence. With no time to develop individual characters, actors were often typecast, playing the same type of character in play after play.

Plays and Playwriting

Shakespeare quickly earned fame and fortune for his hugely popular plays, and the public demand for new plays kept him busy. Shakespeare wrote about two plays each season, often continuing to work on a play while it was being rehearsed for performance.

Appearing at court

S hakespeare's company was always welcome at court and regularly performed for Elizabeth I and later for James I. A temporary stage was built inside one of the royal palaces. The monarch sat on a raised seat, or "state," to watch. Plays were strictly censored by the Revels Office to ensure they did not contain anything that would be offensive to the monarch.

ABOVE: Edward Alleyn, one of the greatest actors of Shakespeare's day

LEFT: A play being acted in court for Queen Elizabeth I

DID YOU KNOW?

The playwright John Fletcher (1579–1625) probably collaborated with Shakespeare on *Henry VIII*, and Shakespeare may have helped with Fletcher's play *The Two Noble Kinsmen*. A third collaboration, *Cardenio*, was performed in 1613, but all written copies have been lost.

Ben Jonson

Rebellion and Richard II

Richard II was probably first performed in front of Queen Elizabeth's chief minister, Sir Robert Cecil, in December 1596. The scene in which the king is deposed by Bolingbroke was thought too sensitive, and cut. In 1601 the Earl of Essex commissioned the Lord Chamberlain's Men to perform the uncensored play, on the day before his planned rebellion against the queen. The rebellion failed, Essex was beheaded, and the Lord Chamberlain's Men were lucky to escape punishment themselves.

Fellow playwrights

Other popular playwrights in Shakespeare's time included:

BEN JONSON (1572–1637)

A leading dramatist, Jonson was also a great friend of Shakespeare's. He, too, started his career as an actor, then turned to writing plays. He was named poet laureate in 1616.

GREATEST WORKS: *Volpone; The Silent Women; The Alchemist*

CHRISTOPHER MARLOWE (1564–1593)

The principal writer for the Rose Theatre, Marlowe wrote many heroic parts for the great actor Edward Alleyn. He was often in trouble with the authorities and was arrested several times. At the age of twenty-nine, he was stabbed to death in a tavern brawl.

GREATEST WORKS: *Tamburlaine; The Jew of Malta; Doctor Faustus*

THOMAS KYD (1558–1594)

The author of *The Spanish Tragedy,* the most popular of Elizabethan tragedies, Kyd set a trend for bloody tales of revenge. He was arrested and tortured for holding unorthodox religious and moral views but was released after implicating his friend Marlowe. He died shortly afterward.

GREATEST WORKS: *The First Part of Hieronimo; The Spanish Tragedy*

Shakespeare Retires

In 1611 or 1612, about a year before the disastrous fire at the Globe, Shakespeare returned to live in Stratford with his family. Although he is thought to have retired from writing, he remained friends with many actors and playwrights, and continued to visit London.

Living in New Place

Shakespeare settled in New Place, a house he bought in 1597. He was now a wealthy man, and New Place was said to be second finest house in Stratford. It was the only house made of brick and had two gardens, two orchards, and two barns. Shakespeare still spent most of his time working in London, but finally settled at New Place in 1610. His elder daughter, Susanna, had married John Hall, a highly respected herbalist and doctor, in 1607. They lived in another fine house, Hall's Croft. His younger daughter, Judith, married Thomas Quiney in 1616.

New Place

Our revels now are ended. These our actors,
As I foretold you, were all spirits, and
Are melted into air, into thin air;
And like the baseless fabric of this vision,
The cloud-capped towers, the gorgeous palaces,
The solemn temples, the great globe itself,
Yea, all which it inherit, shall dissolve
And, like this insubstantial pageant faded,
Leave not a rack behind. We are such stuff
As dreams are made on, and our little life
Is rounded with a sleep.
(*Prospero*, The Tempest, *Act IV, sc. i, 148–158*)

MOURNING RINGS

In his will, Shakespeare left 25 shillings and 8 pence to three of his oldest friends in Stratford and London, to buy mourning rings. It was customary to wear such rings in memory of a dead friend.

Shakespeare's will

Early in 1616, Shakespeare wrote his will, which still survives today. He left most of his estate to Susanna, including New Place, houses in Stratford and London, and the land he had bought outside Stratford. To Judith, he left a large sum of money and his "broad silver-gilt bowl". He left his sister Joan some money, his clothes and the use of the Henley Street house for life. By right, his wife, Anne, received a third of his estate. But Shakespeare also left her "the second best bed", which meant the bed they slept in. The best bed in a house was reserved for guests.

Shakespeare's death

Shakespeare is thought to have died on April 23, 1616, on his 52nd birthday. He was buried two days later in Holy Trinity Church, Stratford.

The Gower memorial to Shakespeare in Stratford

Collected Works

Thirty-eight Shakespeare plays have survived to this day. He also wrote poems, including 154 sonnets and three longer works. While it is hard to know the exact date of each work, scholars have come up with approximate dates by consulting documents of the time.

Saving the plays

Shakespeare had his poems published in his lifetime but not his plays. About half of the plays were printed, unofficially, as small paperback books called quartos. Some quartos were based on notes scribbled down during a performance. When the Globe burned in 1613, the actors rescued many precious costumes, props, and Shakespeare's play scripts. In 1623 the scripts were collected and published as a book, now called the First Folio. It was the first official collection of plays by Shakespeare. More than 200 copies survive.

A list of actors, including Shakespeare himself, printed in the First Folio

ABOVE: *The title page of the* Hamlet *quarto, 1604*

LEFT: *The title page from the First Folio*

DATES OF SHAKESPEARE'S WORKS

◆ PLAYS

1590–1592 *Henry VI, Part 1; Henry VI, Part 2; Henry VI, Part 3*
1592–1593 *The Two Gentlemen of Verona; Richard III*
1592–1594 *The Comedy of Errors*
1593–1594 *Titus Andronicus; The Taming of the Shrew*
1594 *Love's Labour's Lost*
1594–1596 *King John*
1595 *Richard II*
1595–1596 *Romeo and Juliet; A Midsummer Night's Dream*
1596–1597 *The Merchant of Venice; The Merry Wives of Windsor; Henry IV, Part 1*
1598 *Henry IV, Part 2*
1598–1599 *Much Ado About Nothing*

DID YOU KNOW?

In the seventeenth and eighteenth centuries, writers such as Nahum Tate and Colly Cibber rewrote Shakespeare's plays to make them more popular. For example, Tate gave *King Lear* a happy ending, in which Cordelia marries Edgar. (In Shakespeare's original, Cordelia dies.) This version remained the set text for actors for more than 150 years. It was not until the twentieth century that playgoers once again saw *King Lear* and other rewritten plays in their original form.

The Sonnets

Sonnets often tell a love story about real people but with false names. Shakespeare's sonnets, first published in 1609, seem to be about the poet's devotion toward a young man and an older woman known as the Dark Lady. The young man may have been Henry Wriothesley, Earl of Southampton, one of Shakespeare's early patrons. Many sonnets are dedicated to "Mr. W. H.," which may be Wriothesley's initials in reverse. Sonnets are short poems of fourteen lines, with a strict system of rhyming. In each group of four lines, alternate lines rhyme (that is, lines 1 and 3, and lines 2 and 4). The last two lines are a rhyming couplet: They rhyme with each other.

The Earl of Southampton, Shakespeare's patron

A new play

In 1998 a historical play written in the early 1590s was generally acknowledged as being a "lost" play by Shakespeare. *Edward III* tells of the early days of the Hundred Years War between Britain and France. An American computer analysis of the text and language in seven surviving copies convinced most scholars that the play was Shakespeare's work.

The Histories

Shakespeare's history plays present real characters and events in a dramatic way. This means that Shakespeare sometimes altered facts and dates to suit his plot. These plays focus on themes of war, kingship, and the struggle for power.

<table>
<tr><td>THE HISTORY PLAYS</td></tr>
</table>

Henry VI, Parts 1, 2, and *3*
1590–1592
Richard III 1592–1593
King John 1594–1596
Richard II 1595
Henry IV, Part 1 1596–1597
Henry IV, Part 2 1598
Henry V 1599
Henry VIII 1612–1613

The Wars of the Roses

The first group of history plays consists of *Henry VI, Parts 1, 2,* and *3,* and *Richard III.* They cover the period from 1422 to 1485, when the noble houses of Lancaster and York fought for the English throne. The wars are named after their emblems: the white rose of York and the red rose of Lancaster.

*O God! methinks it were a happy life,
To be no better than a homely swain.*
    King Henry, Henry VI, Part 3,
        Act II, sc. v, 21–22

Henry VI, Parts 1, 2, and 3

The three plays about Henry VI look at the problems of weak kingship and the bitter struggle for succession. Henry VI, the Lancastrian King of England and a gentle man, is unable to quash a rebellion masterminded by the Duke of York. To restore peace, he makes York heir to the throne. Civil war follows. York is killed, but his eldest son, Edward, becomes king. Henry is captured and murdered by Edward's brother Richard, who later becomes Richard III.

Henry VI as played by Ralph Fiennes in a 1988 production

ABOVE: In a 1995 film, Ian McKellen's Richard III rules a 1930s fascist state.

RIGHT: Frances Tomalty and Antony Sher in a 1984 RSC production of Richard III. *Richard is usually portrayed as a hunchback, a symbol of evil in Shakespeare's day.*

DID YOU KNOW?

Shakespeare's main source for the history plays was Raphael Holinshed's *Chronicles of England, Scotland, and Ireland,* published in 1577 and revised in 1587. For the early plays he also used *The Union of the Noble and Illustre Families of Lancaster and York* by Edward Hall, which was one of several chronicles commissioned by King Henry VII.

Richard III

As Edward IV lies dying, his evil brother Richard plots his own path to the throne. First he disposes of his rivals. His elder brother, the Duke of Clarence, is sent to the Tower of London and killed. Edward's two young sons are also sent to the Tower and later murdered. Richard is crowned king. On the eve of the Battle of Bosworth Field, however, Richard's past returns to haunt him when his victims' ghosts appear. The next day he is killed by Henry Tudor, Earl of Richmond, who becomes King Henry VII.

The later history plays

Though written later, the second group of history plays (*Richard II; Henry IV, Parts 1* and *2;* and *Henry V*) deals with an earlier period of history. They are set in the years leading up to the Wars of the Roses, 1377 to 1422. Their themes are similar to those in the first set of plays, but Shakespeare placed more emphasis on the emotions of the leading characters.

Richard II

In Shakespeare's time, being king was seen as a sacred duty, given by God. Such power, however, can lead to a king's downfall. Richard is a weak ruler whose arrogance upsets the nobles he depends on. They side instead with his cousin Henry Bolingbroke. As Richard loses his grip on power, a humbler and more sympathetic man emerges. At the end of the play, Richard surrenders his crown to Bolingbroke.

Jeremy Irons as Richard II in the 1986 RSC production

With mine own tears I wash away my balm,
With mine own hands I give away my crown,
With mine own tongue deny my sacred state,
With mine own breath release all duty's rites.
Richard, Richard II, *Act IV, sc. i, 197–200*

> **DID YOU KNOW?**
>
> In the English Shakespeare Company's 1986 modern production of *Henry IV, Parts 1* and *2,* Hal was dressed in tattered jeans. The Boar's Head Tavern, where he drank with Falstaff, was depicted as a pub used by punks and bikers.

Henry IV, Parts 1 and 2

Bolingbroke becomes King Henry IV, whose son, Hal, spends much of his time drinking with his friend Falstaff. When a rebellion begins, Hal must prove himself worthy of the crown. He kills Hotspur, the rebel leader. At the end of *Part 2,* Hal promises his dying father that he is now reformed. When the king dies, Hal is crowned Henry V.

The 1997 RSC production of Henry V *was set in the Second World War.*

Kenneth Branagh played Henry V in the 1989 film version, which he also directed.

Henry V

In *Henry V,* Hal declares war on France. At the Battle of Agincourt, the English are heavily outnumbered, but Hal visits the troops and delivers a famous rallying speech. Against the odds, the English are victorious. Hal is portrayed as a model king and soldier. But he is also aware of the human cost of war and of his own responsibilities as king.

The Comedies

Many of Shakespeare's plays are lighthearted, although even the comedies contain tragedy and passion. Often involving mistaken identity, trickery, or love at first sight, the plots of the comedies can be complicated to follow, but they always have happy endings.

The Taming of the Shrew

This is a play about husbands, wives, and marriage. No one will marry bad-tempered Katherine, the "shrew." Though her younger sister, Bianca, has plenty of suitors, custom says Katherine must be married first. Petruchio offers to marry Katherine, whom he calls Kate, then sets about "taming" her. Eventually, she becomes a dutiful Elizabethan wife.

The Merchant of Venice

Needing money to woo Portia, Bassanio asks his friend Antonio for help. Antonio borrows 3,000 ducats from Shylock, a Jewish moneylender, agreeing that if he does not repay the loan within three months, he must give Shylock a pound of his flesh. A powerful mixture of romance, comedy, and tragedy, the play also looks at the destructive power of racial prejudice.

Fie! fie! unknit that threat'ning unkind brow,
And dart not scornful glances from those eyes
To wound thy lord, thy king, thy governor.
It blots thy beauty, as frosts do bite the meads.
　　Katherine, The Taming of the Shrew, *Act V, sc. ii, 141–144*

Shylock (Antony Sher) and his daughter Jessica (Deborah Goodman) in the 1987 RSC production of The Merchant of Venice

A Midsummer Night's Dream

In *A Midsummer Night's Dream*, Oberon, King of the Fairies, uses a magic love potion to end a quarrel with his wife, Titania, and to solve the problems of four young lovers – but the young people and Titania herself all end up falling in love with the wrong people. By the end of the play, Oberon and his mischievous servant, Puck, have put things right, and a happy ending is assured.

Titania (Claire Higgins) and Bottom (David Troughton), plus faires, in the 1989 RSC production

Much Ado About Nothing

At first, Beatrice and Benedick are too proud to admit that they are in love; their time together is spent arguing and outdoing each other with witticisms. Eventually, after being tricked into revealing their true feelings, they resolve their "merry war" and are married. Meanwhile, Claudio and Hero conduct their own, nearly tragic, romance.

Beatrice (Emma Thompson) and others run to meet the homecoming soldiers in the 1994 film adaptation of Much Ado About Nothing.

As You Like It

The heroine Rosalind falls in love with Orlando, but she is banished from court by her uncle, Duke Frederick. Disguised as a boy called Ganymede, Rosalind and her cousin Celia leave court and enter the Forest of Arden. Orlando is also banished to the forest, where he meets the disguised Rosalind. His brother Oliver falls in love with Celia, and eventually Orlando discovers Ganymede's true identity. The couples are married.

DID YOU KNOW?

In the 1991 Cheek by Jowl production of *As You Like It*, all the parts were played by men. So the actor playing Rosalind was a man playing a woman disguised as a man!

In Christine Edzard's 1992 film version, the Forest of Arden was shown as an inner-city wasteland surrounded by high-rise office buildings that represented the court. As Ganymede, Rosalind wore a woolly hat, a bomber jacket, and jeans.

Corin (Colin Douglas), a shepherd, and Rosalind (Juliet Stevenson) in a production of As You Like It

Some are born great, some achieve greatness, and some have greatness thrust upon them.
Malvolio, Twelfth Night, Act II, sc. v, 132–133

MERRY WIVES

It is thought that Shakespeare wrote *The Merry Wives of Windsor* especially for Queen Elizabeth I because she wanted to see the character of Falstaff (from *Henry IV, Part 1*) in love. Legend says that the play took Shakespeare just fourteen days to write.

The merry wives in this 1985 production act their scene in a hairdresser's salon.

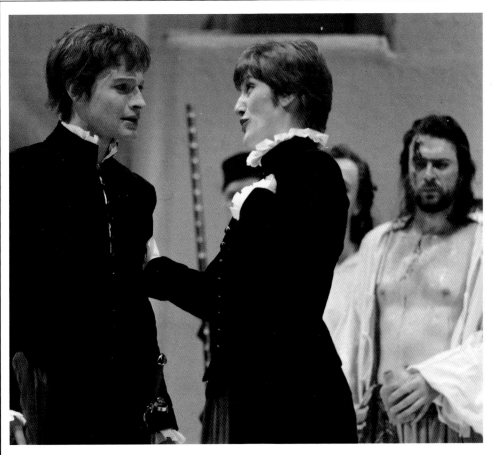

Viola (Harriet Walter) is reunited with Sebastian (Paul Spence) in Twelfth Night.

Twelfth Night

Another romantic comedy of mistaken identity, *Twelfth Night* is set in the imaginary country of Illyria. Viola is shipwrecked, and disguised as a boy called Cesario, she works as a page for Duke Orsino. When Cesario is sent to woo Olivia for his master, Olivia falls in love with Cesario, not Orsino. Meanwhile, Viola's twin brother, Sebastian, arrives in Illyria. Olivia mistakes him for Cesario and marries him. Eventually, all is resolved, and Viola and Orsino are also married.

The Dark Comedies

All's Well That Ends Well, Troilus and Cressida, and *Measure for Measure* are often grouped with the comedies, but the comedy in these plays is much darker. They paint a sometimes disturbing picture of human nature, and the happily-ever-after endings are not all they seem.

> 'Twere all one,
> That I should love a bright
>   particular star
> And think to wed it, he is so above
>   me.
>   *Helena,* All's Well That Ends
>   Well, *Act I, sc. i, 84–86*

All's Well That Ends Well

Helena cures the King of France, who, in thanks, offers her Bertram as a husband. He reluctantly marries her, then leaves to fight the wars in Italy. He tells Helena he will return only if she can get the ring from his finger and have his child, thinking these tasks impossible. She succeeds through trickery. Reunited with Helena, Bertram remains an unwilling husband.

The French King's court in a traditional production of All's Well That Ends Well *by the RSC in 1967*

PLAYING THE FOOL

Fools play an important part in Shakespeare's comedies. They sing, make jokes and puns, and act as messengers for other characters. Feste, the fool in *Twelfth Night*, also turns the tables: His role is to make the audience aware of the foolishness of the main characters. The part was written for Robert Armin, who succeeded William Kempe as chief clown in Shakespeare's company.

Troilus and Cressida

*T*roilus and Cressida is set during the Trojan War. Troilus, a Trojan prince, loves Cressida, but she betrays him for a Greek soldier, Diomedes. Troilus fails to take revenge. The play ends with the murder of Troilus's brother, Hector. Not a comedy, tragedy, or history, *Troilus and Cressida* is a powerful commentary on the futility of love and war.

Time hath, my lord,
A wallet at his back, wherein he puts
Alms for oblivion, a great-sized monster
Of ingratitudes. Those scraps are good deeds past,
Which are devour'd as fast as they are made,
Forgot as soon as done.
  Ulysses, Troilus and Cressida,
    Act III, sc. iii, 139–144

The trial scene, with Derek Griffiths as Pompey, in the RSC's 1994 production of Measure for Measure

Measure for Measure

A play about justice and mercy, *Measure for Measure* is set in Vienna, where Angelo sentences Claudio to death for getting Juliet, Claudio's fiancée, pregnant. Claudio's sister, Isabella, pleads for his life. Angelo asks Isabella to sleep with him, in exchange for Claudio's life. Isabella refuses. Duke Vincentio intervenes, pardons Claudio, and sentences Angelo to death. Isabella then pleads for mercy for Angelo. Moved, Duke Vincentio spares him.

Haste still pays haste, and leisure answers leisure;
Like doth quit like, and measure still for measure.
  Duke, Measure for Measure,
    Act V, sc. i, 408–409

The Tragedies

The tragedies include Shakespeare's most popular and powerful plays. Each one focuses on a tragic hero whose character has a fatal flaw, or weakness, such as jealousy, pride, or indecision. Combined with bad luck, these personal failings inevitably lead to tragic conclusions.

Titus Andronicus

Set in ancient Rome, *Titus Andronicus* is Shakespeare's first and goriest tragedy, a tale of revenge involving Titus, a Roman general, and Tamora, Queen of the Goths. As the play unfolds, Titus's daughter, Lavinia, is raped, and Titus cuts off his own hand in grief. In revenge, Titus kills Tamora's sons and bakes them in a pie, which he serves to their mother.

The pie being presented to Tamora in the 1981 production of Titus Andronicus by the RSC

It was my dear; and he that wounded her
Hath hurt me more than had he killed me dead:
For now I stand as one upon a rock,
Environed with a wilderness of sea.
Titus, Titus Andronicus, Act III, sc. i, 91–94

ROMEO AND JULIET

Some famous spin-offs of *Romeo and Juliet*:

◆ In the hit 1957 musical *West Side Story*, composed by Leonard Bernstein, the Montagues and the Capulets become rival gangs, the Jets and the Sharks. The action is set in New York City.

◆ The Royal Ballet's version of the play, choreographed by Kenneth MacMillan and first performed in 1965 in London, starred Margot Fonteyn as Juliet and Rudolf Nureyev as Romeo.

◆ Baz Luhrmann's extremely successful 1996 film starred Claire Danes and Hollywood superstar Leonardo DiCaprio.

The time is out of joint. O cursèd spite,
That ever I was born to set it right!
Hamlet, Hamlet, *Act I, sc. v,*
189–190

BELOW: Kenneth Branagh as Hamlet in the 1993 production by the RSC

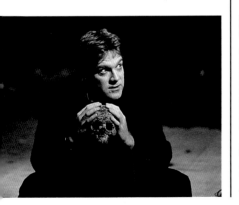

Romeo and Juliet

Romeo and Juliet marry in secret, but their young love is doomed by the bitter feud between their families, the Montagues and the Capulets. They are also victims of a tragic misunderstanding. Juliet's father wants her to marry Paris. She pretends to agree but takes a sleeping potion that makes her appear dead. Romeo finds her and, believing her dead, kills himself. When Juliet wakes and sees his body, she stabs herself to death.

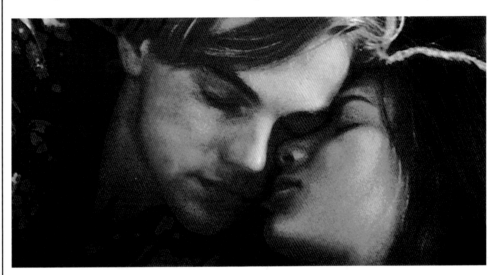

Leonardo DiCaprio and Claire Danes played Romeo and Juliet in the 1996 film.

Hamlet

Hamlet's fatal flaw is indecision. He cannot bring himself to kill his uncle, Claudius, who murdered his father. As he delays, pretending to be insane, Hamlet accidentally kills Polonius, whose daughter, Ophelia, goes mad with grief and drowns. Meanwhile, Claudius tries to kill Hamlet and inadvertently poisons the Queen. Hamlet kills Claudius but is fatally wounded in a duel with Ophelia's brother, Laertes, and dies.

A modern production of Othello, by the RSC

O! beware, my lord, of jealousy. It is the green-eyed monster which doth mock The meat it feeds on.
     Iago, Othello, Act III, sc. iii, 169–171

Othello

In this powerful and moving play, jealousy and issues of race and politics cause a terrible tragedy. Othello, goaded by his friend Iago, becomes convinced that his wife, Desdemona, is having an affair. Eventually his jealousy becomes too much to bear, and he kills her. Too late, he realizes that Iago has lied, and overcome with grief, he stabs himself and dies.

King Lear (Robert Stephens) in the 1993 RSC production

King Lear

King Lear decides to divide his kingdom among his three daughters, according to how much they love him. Cordelia, the most genuinely loving, refuses to take part in the contest and is banished. Her two sisters, Goneril and Regan, reject their father and quarrel among themselves. When Lear finally sees that what he took for real love is false, it is too late. His family and kingdom have been destroyed.

Is this a dagger which I see before me,
The handle toward my hand?
Macbeth, Macbeth, *Act II, sc. i, 33–34*

Macbeth

Driven by ambition and encouraged by his wife, Macbeth murders King Duncan and takes over the throne. He also kills his friend Banquo. But Banquo's ghost appears to haunt him, and Macbeth is tormented by guilt. Then Lady Macbeth kills herself, unable to live with her conscience. A weak man, Macbeth sinks deeper and deeper into evil; yet in the end he faces his own death bravely, as the proud soldier he once was.

The real King Macbeth was very unlike the tragic hero of Shakespeare's play. He ruled Scotland wisely and well from 1040 to 1057. Although he did seize the throne from King Duncan, his claim to the crown was as strong as Duncan's, and Duncan was killed in battle, not murdered by Macbeth.

The 1996 RSC production of Macbeth. *The figures on the right are the three witches.*

The Roman Plays

THE ROMAN PLAYS

Julius Caesar 1599
Antony and Cleopatra
1606–1607
Coriolanus 1607–1608

Also known as the Roman tragedies, these three plays are set in ancient Rome. They examine the problems of power and politics, the responsibilities faced by leaders of state, and the strengths and weaknesses of historical figures.

Julius Caesar

Fearing Julius Caesar's power, a group of Romans, including Caesar's friend Brutus, rebels against him. On the Ides of March (March 15), they murder Caesar in the Senate. Mark Antony plans to avenge his death; in a stirring speech, he turns the crowd against Brutus. Without support, and guilty about his part in Caesar's death, Brutus cannot live with power. At the battle of Philippi, Brutus and Cassius are defeated and kill themselves.

Friends, Romans, countrymen, lend me your ears.
I come to bury Caesar, not to praise him.
The evil that men do lives after them;
The good is oft interrèd with their bones.
  Antony, Julius Caesar, Act III, sc. ii, 74–77

Caesar (Christopher Benjamin) being carried in procession to the Senate in the 1972 RSC production of Julius Caesar

DID YOU KNOW?

The Roman plays show how Shakespeare sometimes altered the truth for dramatic effect. In *Julius Caesar*, set in the first century, a clock strikes (about 1,000 years before clocks were invented), and Cleopatra in *Antony and Cleopatra* plays billiards (a game that was not invented for another 1,500 years).

Antony and Cleopatra

Antony must choose between his duty to Rome and his love for Cleopatra, Queen of Egypt. To settle a quarrel, Antony marries Caesar's sister, Octavia, but returns to Cleopatra. In the war that follows, Caesar defeats Antony at Actium. Hearing a false report of Cleopatra's death, Antony falls on his sword and dies. Rather than give herself up to Rome, Cleopatra kills herself with a bite from a poisonous asp, or snake.

Elizabeth Taylor and Richard Burton in the classic 1963 film Cleopatra

BELOW: Coriolanus returns triumphant with his soldiers, in a production by the RSC.

Coriolanus

The great Roman soldier Coriolanus shows courage and heroism in battle, but these qualities are no preparation for political power. Too proud and snobbish to be a good leader, Coriolanus quickly becomes unpopular. Finally, accused of betraying Rome, he is banished and eventually murdered.

The Late Plays

The plays Shakespeare wrote near the end of his career are romantic comedies. Set in worlds filled with magic and supernatural forces, they focus on characters who are reunited, reconciled, and forgiven for past wrongs.

THE LATE PLAYS

Pericles 1607–1608
Cymbeline 1609–1610
The Winter's Tale 1610–1611
The Tempest 1611

Cymbeline

Cymbeline, King of Britain, has a daughter, Imogen, whose wicked stepmother wants her to marry Cloten, her son. But Imogen secretly marries Posthumus Leonatus.

Thinking Imogen unfaithful, Posthumus orders her killed, but she escapes, disguised as a boy called Fidele. She is reunited with her two long-lost brothers but, thinking Posthumus dead, she joins the Roman invasion of Britain. The Romans are defeated and Fidele is taken prisoner. But "his" life is spared and all is resolved, and Cymbeline is reunited with Imogen and his sons.

A father cruel, and a stepdame false,
A foolish suitor to a wedded lady
That hath her husband banished.
Imogen, Cymbeline,
Act I, sc. vi, 1–3

The Winter's Tale

Perdita, when a baby, is abandoned on the shore of Bohemia on the orders of her father, Leontes, King of Sicily, who, in a jealous rage, believed his wife Hermione had been unfaithful to him. When his wife dies, Leontes repents, but it is too late. Perdita is found and brought up by a shepherd. Sixteen years pass. Perdita falls in love with Florizel, son of Polixenes, King of Bohemia, but the king forbids them to marry. The couple flees to Sicily, where Perdita's true identity is uncovered. It is then revealed that Hermione is still alive, and she is reconciled with her husband and daughter.

Hermione and Leontes reconcile in a 1986 production of The Winter's Tale.

Miranda and Prospero in a 1978 production of The Tempest

O wonder!
How many goodly creatures are there here!
How beauteous mankind is!
O brave new world,
That has such people in't!
Miranda, The Tempest, *Act V, sc. i, 184–187*

The Tempest

Prospero, the Duke of Milan, and his daughter, Miranda, are cast out to sea by Prospero's wicked brother, Antonio. They are stranded on a distant island, where Prospero uses magic to control the spirit Ariel and the monster Caliban. He also raises a magical storm, or tempest, which brings all his old enemies to the island, including his usurping brother, Antonio; the King of Naples, Alonso; and Alonso's son, Ferdinand. Miranda and Ferdinand fall in love and are married. At the end of the play, Prospero gives up magic, forgives his enemies, and sails for home. Some people think that this represented Shakespeare's farewell to writing.

Performing Shakespeare

Each year hundreds of productions of Shakespeare's plays are staged, from those put on by amateur groups to sell-out tours by the world's greatest theatre companies. Each production is unique; each actor, director, and designer brings individual ideas and skills to the plays.

Choosing a play

The director chooses the play and decides how it should be interpreted and staged. It might be performed in modern dress, in authentic Elizabethan costumes, or in an unusual setting. The director works closely with the actors, guiding them in how to speak their lines and move about onstage.

Preparing for a role

The actors decide how to play their parts to suit the director's interpretation. This means they must know their characters inside out, imagining what makes them think and act as they do. Actors do a great deal of research into the roles and often visit places associated with their plays or their characters.

Traditional Elizabethan costumes were worn by Francesca Annis and Barrie Ingham in the 1974 RSC production of Measure for Measure.

A PAGE FROM AN ACTOR'S NOTEBOOK
Character notes are based on those made by the actor Philip Voss.

TITLE OF PLAY: *Twelfth Night*

CHARACTER'S NAME: *Malvolio*

SUPER-OBJECTIVE: *To stop being a servant. He wants to rule. He longs for people to be subservient to him.*

OBJECTIVE: *Advancement socially. To lift himself above his station in life.*

LINE OF ACTION: *To do everything he can to please his mistress by complying with ALL the instructions he reads in the letter.*

OBSTACLES AGAINST IT: *The letter is a fake. He is unbelievably gullible and vain.*

PULSE: *Quick*

PHYSICAL CENTER: *The spine*

OTHER VITAL INFORMATION: *One feels his childhood was a struggle—poor and put upon.*

DID YOU KNOW?

Shakespeare's plays include very few stage directions. The most famous direction comes from *The Winter's Tale*, Act III, scene iii. Antigonus lays Perdita on the shore and then leaves, never to be seen again. The stage direction for Antigonus reads, "Exit, pursued by a bear."

Get your apparel together, good strings to your beards, new ribbons to your pumps. Meet presently at the palace . . . and, most dear actors, eat no onions, nor garlic, for we are to utter sweet breath.
Bottom, A Midsummer Night's Dream, *Act IV, sc. ii, 31–40*

In rehearsal

Rehearsals begin with a read-through of the play. Then the actors work on individual scenes before the whole play is put together. At first the actors read from scripts, but when opening night arrives, they must know their lines by heart. They practice in a rehearsal room, not on the stage, and often wear casual clothes while the set and costumes are being designed and made. About a week before the premiere, a technical rehearsal is held to check scene changes and lighting. This is followed by the dress rehearsal in full costume, which is the last chance to make any changes before the curtain rises on opening night.

A young cast rehearses for the RSC production of The Winter's Tale *in 1998.*

LEFT: A modern set design for Romeo and Juliet *at the Royal Shakespeare Theatre in Stratford, England*

BELOW: Backstage in the RSC wardrobe department

Behind the scenes

Producing a Shakespeare play is a huge undertaking. Here are a few key members of the backstage team:

STAGE MANAGER: In charge of the actual performances once the play opens; looks after everything on the stage

ASSISTANT STAGE MANAGER: Does a bit of everything: finds props, prompts, and makes sure that the actors are in their correct positions

SET DESIGNER: Designs scenery and stage sets

WARDROBE DEPARTMENT: Designs, makes, and takes care of the costumes

DRESSER: Helps the actors get into their costumes

STAGEHANDS: Put up, take down, and move the scenery

TECHNICIANS: Control lighting and sound

ORIGINAL MUSIC

The only pieces of original music to survive from any of Shakespeare's plays are those for Feste's songs in *Twelfth Night*. These were set on paper by Thomas Morley.

Setting the scene

Set design, lighting, costumes, and props all help to create a particular setting and atmosphere. There is no one correct way of setting the background for Shakespeare, and there have been both traditional and modern adaptations of all of Shakespeare's plays. Working from the director's vision, the set designer makes a model of the set; then the set building begins. The lighting and props must also fit the design.

Dressing the part

Costumes help set the scene and communicate the personalities of the characters. For example, in the 1993 production of *The Merchant of Venice,* the play was set in a dealing room in the City of London (the financial district), and cast members were dressed as City financiers. To get used to wearing costumes, the actors might wear something similar during rehearsals. At the dress rehearsal, they don performance costumes.

Some unusual costumes and makeup in a 1983 production of The Comedy of Errors *by the RSC*

Shakespeare in Company

Almost 400 years after Shakespeare's death, his plays are still hugely popular all over the world. Many countries have theatres and companies dedicated to Shakespeare's work, and some hold annual Shakespeare festivals.

The Royal Shakespeare Company (RSC)

The world-famous RSC has three theatres in Stratford-upon-Avon, Shakespeare's birthplace. The largest is the Royal Shakespeare Theatre, opened on April 23, 1932, Shakespeare's birthday. The Barbican Theatre is the RSC's London home. There are two companies, each of about eighty actors, that play in Stratford and London, and take plays on national and world tours. They operate on a repertory system, which means that in a single season, actors take on several roles in a range of plays.

The Swan Theatre in Stratford. The RSC also has a third studio theatre, called The Other Place.

ABOVE: The Royal Shakespeare Theatre in Stratford at night

ON THE NET

If you have access to the Internet, you can find out much more about Shakespeare and his plays. You can try the following sites:
www.rsc.org.uk
www.shakespeare.org.uk
www.romeoandjuliet.com

THE OTHER RSC

The Reduced Shakespeare Company, which began touring in the early 1980s, presents fast, furious, and funny versions of all of Shakespeare's plays in just under two hours. The plays are peformed in different styles; for example, *Othello* becomes a rap number.

The Old Globe Theatre in San Diego, California

Francesca Annis (left) and Judi Dench (right) in the 1976 RSC production of The Comedy of Errors

Shakespeare around the world

There are Shakespeare theatres all over the world, including replicas of the Globe in the United States, Japan, and New Zealand. The Australian and New Zealand Shakespeare Association organizes Shakespeare conferences, lectures, workshops, and master classes. In Canada, a Shakespeare Festival is held each year in Stratford, Ontario. Annual festivals also occur throughout the United States.

A production of Hamlet *by a Japanese company, directed by Yukio Ninagawa in London in 1998*

Famous actors

Many actors have became famous by playing Shakespearean roles. The greatest actor of the eighteenth century was David Garrick (1717–1779). In 1769 he initiated the Shakespeare Jubilee in Stratford-upon-Avon, establishing the town as a tourist attraction. In the late nineteenth century, Ellen Terry (1848–1928) starred in the leading female roles. Great Shakespearean stars of the twentieth century include Laurence Olivier, John Gielgud, Derek Jacobi, Peggy Ashcroft, and Judi Dench.

The Speeches on the CD

Here are transcripts of the speeches that can be found on the CD. You can follow the speeches as you listen to them.

HAMLET, ACT III, SC. II, 1–8

HAMLET: Speak the speech, I pray you, as I pronounced it to you—trippingly, on the tongue; but if you mouth it, as many of our players do, I had as lief the town-crier spoke my lines. Nor do not saw the air too much with your hand, thus, but use all gently; for in the very torrent, tempest, and, as I may say, whirlwind of your passion, you must acquire and beget a temperance that may give it smoothness.

AS YOU LIKE IT, ACT II, SC. VII, 139–166

JAQUES: All the world's a stage,
And all the men and women merely
    players.
They have their exits and their entrances,
And one man in his time plays many
    parts,
His acts being seven ages. At first the
    infant,
Mewling and puking in the nurse's arms,
Then the whining schoolboy, with his
    satchel
And shining morning face, creeping like
    a snail
Unwillingly to school. And then the lover,
Sighing like furnace, with a woeful ballad
Made to his mistress' eyebrow. Then a
    soldier,
Full of strange oaths and bearded like the
    pard,
Jealous in honour, sudden and quick in
    quarrel,
Seeking the bubble reputation
Even in the cannon's mouth. And then the
    justice,
In fair round belly with good capon lined,
With eyes severe and beard of formal cut,
Full of wise saws and modern instances;
And so he plays his part. The sixth age
    shifts
Into the lean and slippered pantaloon,
With spectacles on nose and pouch on
    side,
His youthful hose, well saved, a world too
    wide
For his shrunk shank, and his big manly
    voice,
Turning again toward childish treble, pipes
And whistles in his sound. Last scene of
    all,
That ends this strange, eventful history,
Is second childishness and mere oblivion,
Sans teeth, sans eyes, sans taste, sans
    everything.

ROMEO AND JULIET, ACT II, SC. I, 44–91

ROMEO: But soft. What light through
    yonder window breaks?
It is the east, and Juliet is the sun.
Arise, fair sun, and kill the envious moon,
Who is already sick and pale with grief
That thou, her maid, art far more fair
    than she.
Be not her maid, since she is envious.
Her vestal livery is but sick and green,
And none but fools do wear it; cast it off.
It is my lady; O, it is my love.
O that she knew she were!
She speaks, yet she says nothing. What of
    that?
Her eye discourses; I will answer it.
I am too bold. 'Tis not to me she speaks.
Two of the fairest stars in all the heaven,
Having some business, do entreat her
    eyes
To twinkle in their spheres till they return.
What if her eyes were there, they in her
    head?—
The brightness of her cheek would shame
    those stars
As daylight doth a lamp; her eyes in
    heaven
Would through the airy region stream so
    bright
That birds would sing and think it were
    not night.
See how she leans her cheek upon her
    hand!
O that I were a glove upon that hand
That I might touch that cheek!
JULIET: Ay me!
ROMEO: She speaks. O, speak again, bright
    angel; for thou art
As glorious to this night, being o'er my
    head,
As is a wingèd messenger of heaven
Unto the white-upturnèd wond'ring eyes
Of mortals that fall back to gaze on him
When he bestrides the lazy-puffing clouds
And sails upon the bosom of the air.
JULIET: O Romeo, Romeo, wherefore art
    thou Romeo?
Deny thy father and refuse thy name,
Or, if thou wilt not, be but sworn my
    love
And I'll no longer be a Capulet.
ROMEO: Shall I hear more, or shall I speak
    at this?

JULIET: 'Tis but thy name that is my enemy.
Thou art thyself, though not a Montague.
What's Montague? It is nor hand, nor foot,
Nor arm, nor face, nor any other part
Belonging to a man. O, be some other
    name!
What's in a name? That which we call a
    rose
By any other name would smell as sweet,
So Romeo would, were he not Romeo
    called,
Retain that dear perfection which he
    owes
Without that title. Romeo, doff thy name,
And for that name—which is no part of
    thee—
Take all myself.

HENRY V, ACT III, SC. I, 1–34

KING HARRY: Once more unto the breach,
    dear friends, once more,
Or close the wall up with our English
    dead.
In peace there's nothing so becomes a
    man
As modest stillness and humility,
But when the blast of war blows in our
    ears,
Then imitate the action of the tiger.
Stiffen the sinews, summon up the blood,
Disguise fair nature with hard-favoured
    rage.
Then lend the eye a terrible aspect;
Let it pry through the portage of the head
Like the brass cannon; let the brow
    o'erwhelm it
As fearfully as doth a gallèd rock
O'erhang and jutty his confounded base,
Swilled with the wild and wasteful ocean.
Now set the teeth and stretch the nostril
    wide,
Hold hard the breath, and bend up every
    spirit

To his full height. On, on, you noblest
    English,
Whose blood is fet from fathers of war-
    proof,
Fathers that like so many Alexanders
Have in these parts from morn till even
    fought,
And sheathed their swords for lack of
    argument.
Dishonour not your mothers; now attest
That those whom you called fathers did
    beget you.
Be copy now to men of grosser blood,
And teach them how to war. And you,
    good yeomen,
Whose limbs were made in England,
    show us here
The mettle of your pasture; let us swear
That you are worth your breeding—
    which I doubt not,
For there is none of you so mean and
    base
That hath not noble lustre in your eyes.
I see you stand like greyhounds in the
    slips,
Straining upon the start. The game's afoot.
Follow your spirit, and upon this charge
Cry, "God for Harry, England, and Saint
    George!"

RICHARD III, ACT I, SC. I, 1–40

RICHARD GLOUCESTER: Now is the winter of
    our discontent
Made glorious summer by this sun of
    York;
And all the clouds that loured upon our
    house
In the deep bosom of the ocean buried.
Now are our brows bound with victorious
    wreaths,
Our bruisèd arms hung up for monuments,
Our stern alarums changed to merry
    meetings,

Our dreadful marches to delightful
    measures.
Grim-visaged war hath smoothed his
    wrinkled front,
And now, instead of mounting barbèd
    steeds
To fright the souls of fearful adversaries—
He capers, nimbly, in a lady's chamber,
To the lascivious pleasing of a lute.
But I, that am not shaped for sportive
    tricks,
Nor made to court an amorous looking-
    glass,
I, that am rudely stamped and want love's
    majesty
To strut before a wanton ambling nymph,
I, that am curtailed of this fair proportion,
Cheated of feature by dissembling nature,
Deformed, unfinished, sent before my time
Into this breathing world scarce half made
    up—
And that so lamely and unfashionable
That dogs bark at me as I halt by them—
Why, I, in this weak piping time of peace,
Have no delight to pass away the time,
Unless to spy my shadow in the sun
And descant on mine own deformity.
And therefore, since I cannot prove a
    lover,
To entertain these fair well-spoken days,
I am determined to prove a villain
And hate the idle pleasures of these days.
Plots have I laid, inductions dangerous,
By drunken prophecies, libels, and
    dreams,
To set my brother Clarence and the King
Into deadly hate, the one against the other.
And if King Edward be as true and just
As I am subtle, false, and treacherous,
This day should Clarence closely be
    mewed up
About a prophecy which says that "G"
Of Edward's heirs the murderer shall be.

HAMLET, ACT III, SC. I, 58–90

HAMLET: To be, or not to be; that is the
    question:
Whether 'tis nobler in the mind to suffer
The slings and arrows of outrageous
    fortune,
Or to take arms against a sea of troubles,
And, by opposing, end them. To die, to
    sleep
No more, and by a sleep to say we end
The heartache and the thousand natural
    shocks
That flesh is heir to—'tis a consummation
Devoutly to be wished. To die, to sleep.
To sleep, perchance to dream. Ay, there's
    the rub,
For in that sleep of death what dreams
    may come
When we have shuffled off this mortal coil
Must give us pause. For there's the respect
That makes calamity of so long life,
For who would bear the whips and scorns
    of time,
The oppressor's wrong, the proud man's
    contumely,
The pangs of despisèd love, the law's
    delay,
The insolence of office, the spurns
That patient merit of th'unworthy takes,
When he himself might his quietus make
With a bare bodkin? For who would
    fardels bear
To grunt and sweat under a weary life,
But that the dread of something after
    death,
The undiscovered country from whose
    bourn
No traveller returns, puzzles the will,
And makes us rather bear those ills we
    have
Than fly to others that we know not of?
Thus conscience does make cowards of
    us all,
And thus the native hue of resolution
Is sicklied o'er with the pale cast of
    thought,
And enterprises of great pitch and moment
With this regard their currents turn awry,
And lose the name of action.

SONNET 18

Shall I compare thee to a summer's day?
Thou art more lovely and more temperate.
Rough winds do shake the darling buds of
    May,
And summer's lease hath all too short a
    date.
Sometimes too hot the eye of heaven
    shines,
And often is his gold complexion
    dimmed,
And every fair from fair some time
    declines,
By chance or nature's changing course
    untrimmed;
But thy eternal summer shall not fade
Nor lose possession of that fair thou
    ow'st,
Nor shall death brag thou wander'st in his
    shade
When in eternal lines to time thou grow'st.
    So long as men can breathe or eyes
      can see,
    So long lives this, and this give life
      to thee.

SONNET 60

Like as the waves make towards the
    pebbled shore,
So do our minutes hasten to their end,
Each changing place with that which goes
    before;
In sequent toil all forwards do contend.
Nativity, once in the main of light,
Crawls to maturity, wherewith being
    crowned

Crookèd eclipses 'gainst his glory fight,
And time that gave doth now his gift
    confound.
Time doth transfix the flourish set on
    youth,
And delves the parallels in beauty's brow;
Feeds on the rarities of nature's truth,
And nothing stands but for his scythe to
    mow.
    And yet to times in hope my verse
      shall stand,
    Praising thy worth, despite his cruel
      hand.

A MIDSUMMER NIGHT'S DREAM, EPILOGUE

PUCK: If we shadows have offended,
Think but this, and all is mended:
That you have but slumbered here
While these visions did appear;
And this weak and idle theme,
No more yielding but a dream,
Gentles, do not reprehend.
If you pardon, we will mend.
And, as I am an honest Puck,
If we have unearnèd luck
Now to 'scape the serpent's tongue,
We will make amends ere long,
Else the Puck a liar call.
So, good night unto you all.
Give me your hands, if we be friends,
And Robin shall restore amends.

Index

Acknowledgments

Many thanks to Kathy Elgin at the RSC for her help in the production of this book and for acting as a consultant on the text and pictures. As the result of her help, many of the images show many of the RSC's most famous faces in action. Thanks also to Nick Shires for producing the CD and to Jo Fletcher-Watson in her unstinting effort in project-editing the book and obtaining the best imagery possible.

The publisher would like to thank all those who supplied photographs for this book. The copyright owners are listed below:
Donald Cooper c/o Royal Shakespeare Theatre: 37 (left), 38 (right)
Donald Cooper/Photostage: 2, 31
Hulton Getty: 12 (right), 14b, 16, 20 (left)
Jarrold Publishing: 10 (left), 11, 22, 23, 48 (right)
Joe Cocks Studio Collection/Shakespeare Centre Library: 28
John Tramper c/o Shakespeare's Globe: 6, 18
Jonathan Docker-Drysdale, 1998: 45
Manuel Rivas/Old Globe Theatre, San Diego: 49 (top left)
Kobal Collection: 27 (left), 29 (left)
Renaissance Films/Kobal Collection: 32 (left)
Twentieth Century Fox/Kobal Collection: 37 (right), 41 (right)
Museum of London: 12 (left), 14 (top)
C. Walter Hodges/Museum of London: 13 (left), 13 (right), 17
By courtesy of the National Portrait Gallery, London: 8, 9 (right)
Alastair Muir/Open Air Theatre, Regents Park: 56
Pentagram Design Limited: 15
Press Office, Barbican Centre: 49 (middle)
Press Office, Royal Shakespeare Theatre: 48 (left)
Royal Shakespeare Theatre: 32 (right), 34, 35, 39, 42, 43, 44,
46 (right), 49 (bottom left)
Shakespeare Birthplace Trust Museum: 9 (left)
Shakespeare Birthplace Trust Records Office: 10 (right)
Shakespeare Birthplace Trust: endpapers, case
Shakespeare Centre Library: 19 (left), 19 (right), 21, 24 (all), 25, 26, 27 (right),
29 (right), 30, 33 (left), 33 (right), 36, 38 (left), 47
Simon McBride 1991 c/o Royal Shakespeare Theatre: 46 (left)
The Trustees of Dulwich Picture Gallery: 20 (right)
Tom Holte Theatre Photographic Collection/Shakespeare Centre Library: 40, 41 (left)

ENDPIECE: A scene from the 1989 RSC production of A Midsummer Night's Dream